GW01454261

Thandee ♥ Jaymee

Copyright © 2020 by Thandee & Jaymee

All rights reserved. No part of this book may be reproduced without written permission of the copyright owner, except for the use of limited quotations for the purpose of book reviews.

Presented to:

_____

_____

Having You on our Team makes all the Difference.
Thanks for all You Do.

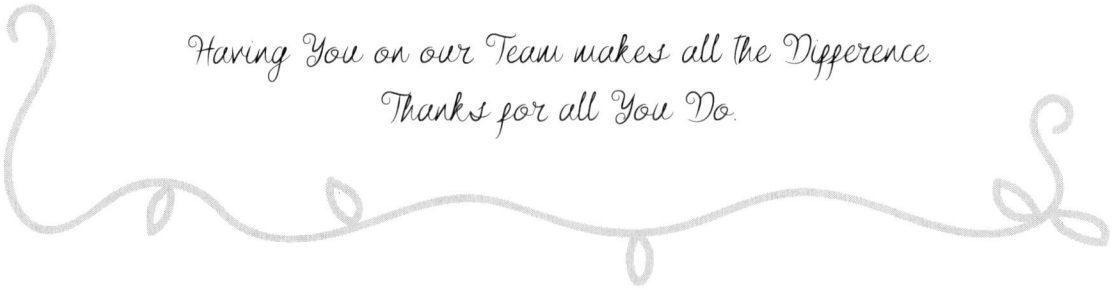

ALL IS WELL

_____

_____

_____

_____

_____

_____

_____

_____

_____

_____

_____

_____

_____

_____

TODAY I'M GRATEFUL FOR

Always be yourself

ALWAYS DELIVER QUALITY

TODAY I'M GRATEFUL FOR

Appreciate the moment

TODAY I'M GRATEFUL FOR

Audit your mistakes

_____

_____

_____

_____

_____

_____

_____

_____

_____

_____

_____

_____

_____

_____

_____

Today I'm grateful for

BE A GIVER

BE A GOAL GETTER!

_____

_____

_____

_____

_____

_____

_____

_____

_____

_____

_____

_____

_____

_____

_____

_____

TODAY I'M GRATEFUL FOR

BE CONSTANTLY CURIOUS

TODAY I'M GRATEFUL FOR

Be here now

_____

TODAY I'M GRATEFUL FOR

BE THE CHANGE

_____

_____

_____

_____

_____

_____

_____

_____

_____

_____

_____

_____

_____

_____

_____

TODAY I'M GRATEFUL FOR

Be the best version of you!

_____

_____

_____

_____

_____

_____

_____

_____

_____

_____

_____

_____

_____

_____

_____

_____

TODAY I'M GRATEFUL FOR

Be obsessively grateful

_____

_____

_____

_____

_____

_____

_____

_____

_____

_____

_____

_____

_____

_____

_____

_____

_____

TODAY I'M GRATEFUL FOR

BELIEVE IN YOURSELF

_____

_____

_____

_____

_____

_____

_____

_____

_____

_____

_____

_____

_____

_____

_____

_____

TODAY I'M GRATEFUL FOR

BELIEVE YOU CAN

_____

_____

_____

_____

_____

_____

_____

_____

_____

_____

_____

_____

_____

_____

_____

_____

TODAY I'M GRATEFUL FOR

BLOCK OUT HATERS

_____

_____
_____
_____
_____
_____
_____
_____
_____
_____
_____
_____
_____
_____
_____
_____
_____

TODAY I'M GRATEFUL FOR

Brainstorm alternative ideas

TODAY I'M GRATEFUL FOR

BRANDING IS ESSENTIAL

TODAY I'M GRATEFUL FOR

BUILD QUALITY RELATIONSHIPS

_____

_____

_____

_____

_____

_____

_____

_____

_____

_____

_____

_____

_____

_____

_____

TODAY I'M GRATEFUL FOR

Build strategic partnerships

TODAY I'M GRATEFUL FOR

Celebrate all success

TODAY I'M GRATEFUL FOR

COMMUNICATE WITH CLARITY

_____

_____

_____

_____

_____

_____

_____

_____

_____

_____

_____

_____

_____

_____

TODAY I'M GRATEFUL FOR

Competition fuels growth

TODAY I'M GRATEFUL FOR

CONQUER FROM WITHIN

TODAY I'M GRATEFUL FOR

CONNECTION BUILDS TRUST

_____

_____

_____

_____

_____

_____

_____

_____

_____

_____

_____

_____

_____

_____

_____

_____

_____

_____

TODAY I'M GRATEFUL FOR

COUNT YOUR BLESSINGS

_____

_____

_____

_____

_____

_____

_____

_____

_____

_____

_____

_____

_____

_____

_____

TODAY I'M GRATEFUL FOR

DARE TO SUCK

_____

_____
_____
_____
_____
_____
_____
_____
_____
_____
_____
_____
_____
_____
_____
_____

TODAY I'M GRATEFUL FOR

DO IT NOW

_____

_____
_____
_____
_____
_____
_____
_____
_____
_____
_____
_____
_____
_____
_____
_____

TODAY I'M GRATEFUL FOR

DREAMS COME TRUE

TODAY I'M GRATEFUL FOR

Embrace constant change

_____

_____

_____

_____

_____

_____

_____

_____

_____

_____

_____

_____

_____

_____

_____

_____

TODAY I'M GRATEFUL FOR

ENJOY LIFE

TODAY I'M GRATEFUL FOR

Every moment matters

TODAY I'M GRATEFUL FOR

Exceptional makes memorable

TODAY I'M GRATEFUL FOR

Exclusivity adds value

TODAY I'M GRATEFUL FOR

FEED YOUR SOUL

_____

_____

_____

_____

_____

_____

_____

_____

_____

_____

_____

_____

_____

_____

_____

_____

TODAY I'M GRATEFUL FOR

FOCUS AND WIN

_____

_____

_____

_____

_____

_____

_____

_____

_____

_____

_____

_____

_____

_____

_____

TODAY I'M GRATEFUL FOR

FRIENDS ARE TREASURES

TODAY I'M GRATEFUL FOR

GOOD VIBES ONLY

_____

_____
_____
_____
_____
_____
_____
_____
_____
_____
_____
_____
_____
_____
_____
_____
_____

TODAY I'M GRATEFUL FOR

_____

_____

_____

_____

_____

_____

_____

_____

_____

_____

_____

_____

_____

_____

_____

_____

_____

TODAY I'M GRATEFUL FOR

Go for it

_____

_____

_____

_____

_____

_____

_____

_____

_____

_____

_____

_____

_____

_____

_____

_____

TODAY I'M GRATEFUL FOR

Handle breakdowns immediately

_____

_____

_____

_____

_____

_____

_____

_____

_____

_____

_____

_____

_____

_____

_____

_____

_____

_____

_____

_____

_____

TODAY I'M GRATEFUL FOR

Happiness is Choice

TODAY I'M GRATEFUL FOR

HEALTH IS WEALTH

_____

_____
_____
_____
_____
_____
_____
_____
_____
_____
_____
_____
_____
_____
_____

TODAY I'M GRATEFUL FOR

HOPE TRUMPS ALL

_____

_____

_____

_____

_____

_____

_____

_____

_____

_____

_____

_____

_____

_____

_____

TODAY I'M GRATEFUL FOR

I'M DETERMINED

TODAY I'M GRATEFUL FOR

Identify key milestones

_____

_____
_____
_____
_____
_____
_____
_____
_____
_____
_____
_____
_____
_____
_____
_____

TODAY I'M GRATEFUL FOR

IT IS POSSIBLE

_____

_____
_____
_____
_____
_____
_____
_____
_____
_____
_____
_____
_____
_____
_____
_____
_____

TODAY I'M GRATEFUL FOR

JUST BE AWESOME

_____

_____

_____

_____

_____

_____

_____

_____

_____

_____

_____

_____

_____

_____

TODAY I'M GRATEFUL FOR

KEEP IT COOL

TODAY I'M GRATEFUL FOR

KEEP MOVING FORWARD

_____

_____

_____

_____

_____

_____

_____

_____

_____

_____

_____

_____

_____

_____

_____

_____

_____

TODAY I'M GRATEFUL FOR

Keep morale high

TODAY I'M GRATEFUL FOR

KEEP ON SHINING!

_____

_____

_____

_____

_____

_____

_____

_____

_____

_____

_____

_____

_____

_____

_____

_____

_____

TODAY I'M GRATEFUL FOR

KEEP THE FAITH

TODAY I'M GRATEFUL FOR

Laughter and Blessings

TODAY I'M GRATEFUL FOR

LAUGHTER IS BEST

_____

_____
_____
_____
_____
_____
_____
_____
_____
_____
_____
_____
_____
_____
_____
_____

TODAY I'M GRATEFUL FOR

Laughter is medicine

_____

_____

_____

_____

_____

_____

_____

_____

_____

_____

_____

_____

_____

_____

TODAY I'M GRATEFUL FOR

LEADERS ARE EARLY

_____

_____

_____

_____

_____

_____

_____

_____

_____

_____

_____

_____

_____

_____

_____

TODAY I'M GRATEFUL FOR

LEARN FROM YESTERDAY

TODAY I'M GRATEFUL FOR

LIFE IS AWESOME

_____

_____

_____

_____

_____

_____

_____

_____

_____

_____

_____

_____

_____

_____

_____

_____

TODAY I'M GRATEFUL FOR

LIFE WON'T WAIT

_____

_____
_____
_____
_____
_____
_____
_____
_____
_____
_____
_____
_____
_____
_____

TODAY I'M GRATEFUL FOR

LIVE LIFE DAILY

TODAY I'M GRATEFUL FOR

LIVE, LOVE, LAUGH

_____

_____
_____
_____
_____
_____
_____
_____
_____
_____
_____
_____
_____
_____
_____

TODAY I'M GRATEFUL FOR

Live your potential

_____

_____

_____

_____

_____

_____

_____

_____

_____

_____

_____

_____

_____

_____

_____

_____

_____

TODAY I'M GRATEFUL FOR

MAINTAIN YOUR INTEGRITY

TODAY I'M GRATEFUL FOR

MANAGE YOUR REPUTATION

_____

_____

_____

_____

_____

_____

_____

_____

_____

_____

_____

_____

_____

_____

TODAY I'M GRATEFUL FOR

MANAGE RESOURCES EFFECTIVELY

_____

_____

_____

_____

_____

_____

_____

_____

_____

_____

_____

_____

_____

_____

_____

TODAY I'M GRATEFUL FOR

MASTERY ABHORS MEDIOCRITY

_____

_____
_____
_____
_____
_____
_____
_____
_____
_____
_____
_____
_____
_____
_____
_____

TODAY I'M GRATEFUL FOR

MODEL THE MASTERS

_____

_____
_____
_____
_____
_____
_____
_____
_____
_____
_____
_____
_____
_____
_____
_____

TODAY I'M GRATEFUL FOR

MONEY AMPLIFIES EMOTIONS

TODAY I'M GRATEFUL FOR

MONITOR BUDGETS REGULARLY

_____

_____

_____

_____

_____

_____

_____

_____

_____

_____

_____

_____

_____

_____

_____

_____

TODAY I'M GRATEFUL FOR

NEVER GIVE UP

TODAY I'M GRATEFUL FOR

NEVER LOOK BACK

TODAY I'M GRATEFUL FOR

NOTHING IS IMPOSSIBLE

_____

_____

_____

_____

_____

_____

_____

_____

_____

_____

_____

_____

_____

_____

_____

_____

_____

TODAY I'M GRATEFUL FOR

NOW OR NEVER

_____

_____

_____

_____

_____

_____

_____

_____

_____

_____

_____

_____

_____

_____

_____

_____

TODAY I'M GRATEFUL FOR

NURTURE YOUR BEST

_____

_____

_____

_____

_____

_____

_____

_____

_____

_____

_____

_____

_____

_____

TODAY I'M GRATEFUL FOR

Passion is enrolling

TODAY I'M GRATEFUL FOR

Peace, love & happiness

_____

_____

_____

_____

_____

_____

_____

_____

_____

_____

_____

_____

_____

_____

TODAY I'M GRATEFUL FOR

Perfectionism stalls progress

TODAY I'M GRATEFUL FOR

PRIORITIZE ALL TASKS

TODAY I'M GRATEFUL FOR

REDUCE YOUR OVERHEADS

_____

_____

_____

_____

_____

_____

_____

_____

_____

_____

_____

_____

_____

_____

TODAY I'M GRATEFUL FOR

REMEMBER TO LIVE

TODAY I'M GRATEFUL FOR

REWARD HIGH PERFORMANCE

_____

_____

_____

_____

_____

_____

_____

_____

_____

_____

_____

_____

_____

_____

TODAY I'M GRATEFUL FOR

Seize the day

_____

_____

_____

_____

_____

_____

_____

_____

_____

_____

_____

_____

_____

_____

_____

_____

TODAY I'M GRATEFUL FOR

Set clear targets

_____

_____
_____
_____
_____
_____
_____
_____
_____
_____
_____
_____
_____
_____
_____
_____
_____
_____
_____

TODAY I'M GRATEFUL FOR

SETTLE YOUR DEBTS

TODAY I'M GRATEFUL FOR

Speak the truth

_____

_____
_____
_____
_____
_____
_____
_____
_____
_____
_____
_____
_____
_____

TODAY I'M GRATEFUL FOR

STOP UNDERESTIMATING YOURSELF

_____

_____
_____
_____
_____
_____
_____
_____
_____
_____
_____
_____
_____
_____
_____
_____
_____

TODAY I'M GRATEFUL FOR

Success breeds success

_____

_____

_____

_____

_____

_____

_____

_____

_____

_____

_____

_____

_____

_____

TODAY I'M GRATEFUL FOR

SUCCESS IS YOURS

TODAY I'M GRATEFUL FOR

TAKE THE RISK

TODAY I'M GRATEFUL FOR

Teamwork makes the dream work

_____

_____

_____

_____

_____

_____

_____

_____

_____

_____

_____

_____

_____

TODAY I'M GRATEFUL FOR

TIME HEALS EVERYTHING

_____

_____
_____
_____
_____
_____
_____
_____
_____
_____
_____
_____
_____
_____

TODAY I'M GRATEFUL FOR

THINK OUTSIDE THE BOX

TODAY I'M GRATEFUL FOR

Track all progress

_____

_____

_____

_____

_____

_____

_____

_____

_____

_____

_____

_____

_____

_____

_____

TODAY I'M GRATEFUL FOR

VALUE YOUR TIME

TODAY I'M GRATEFUL FOR

WINNERS NEVER QUIT

_____

_____
_____
_____
_____
_____
_____
_____
_____
_____
_____
_____
_____
_____
_____
_____
_____

TODAY I'M GRATEFUL FOR

Yes, you can!

_____

TODAY I'M GRATEFUL FOR

You're awesome and I know it!

_____

_____

_____

_____

_____

_____

_____

_____

_____

_____

_____

_____

_____

_____

_____

TODAY I'M GRATEFUL FOR

YOU'VE GOT THIS!

TODAY I'M GRATEFUL FOR

Printed in Great Britain
by Amazon

55558690R00059